Super Science

Plants

Richard Robinson

QED Publishing

First published in the UK in 2007 by
QED Publishing
A Quarto Group company
226 City Road
London EC1V 2TT
www.qed-publishing.co.uk

A catalogue record for this book is available from the British Library.

ISBN 978 1 84538 665 8

Written by Richard Robinson   Publisher Steve Evans
Edited by Anna Claybourne   Creative Director Zeta Davies
Designed by Balley Design Ltd   Senior Editor Hannah Ray
Consultant Terry Jennings

Printed and bound in China

Picture credits
Key: T = top, B = bottom, C = centre, L = left, R = right, FC = front cover

Alamy: p24 Stock Connection.
Corbis: p4 Lester V. Bergman; p17 Danny Cardona/Reuters; p29 Ecoscene.
Getty Images: p7 Louie Psihoyos/Science Faction; p26 Craig Pershouse/Lonely Planet Images.
Science Photo Library: p8, p12 Dr.Jeremy Burgess; p10 Andrew Syred; p14 Sidney Moulds; p15
Dr. Keith Wheeler; p18 Eye of Science; p23 Gregory Dimijian; p25 Sheila Terry; p28 David R. Frazier.

Words in **bold** can be found in
the Glossary on page 31.

Contents

The first plants

Three and a half thousand million years ago, the early Earth was a very hot, smelly place, covered with volcanoes and acidic pools. Among the few life forms that existed were tiny, single-celled things called **cyanobacteria**. They were able to use the light from the Sun to grow and reproduce. These tiny **bacteria** were the early ancestors of plants.

The plants appear

Over millions of years, cyanobacteria joined with other cells to make larger living things, which also used the Sun's light to give them energy and food. These were the first true plants. Plants evolved, changed, and spread across the land, until eventually they covered the planet. Today, there are few places where plants do not exist, and every single plant is descended from the tiny cyanobacteria.

Right: Cyanobacteria are still around today, living in oceans and ponds all over the planet.

Early Earth

Early plants developed the ability to take in **carbon dioxide** gas and use it to help them grow, in a process called **photosynthesis**. They made **oxygen** gas as a waste product.

Little by little, the amount of carbon dioxide in the atmosphere fell, and the amount of oxygen started to rise.

Above: Plants cover over 50% of the Earth's land surface.

A present from the plants

If you had visited the planet when plants first appeared, you would not have liked breathing the air. There was very little oxygen, but there was a lot of another gas, carbon dioxide. In sunlight, plants absorb (take in) carbon dioxide and give out oxygen. Human beings and other animals need oxygen. Plants create an **atmosphere** that we can breathe.

Carbon dioxide is also a 'greenhouse gas' – it makes the atmosphere heat up. So we have to thank plants again. When they changed the balance of the atmosphere, removing carbon dioxide and adding more oxygen, the Earth became cool enough for animals and humans to survive.

Have you noticed any plants in unusual places? See page 30.

Above: If sunflowers went scuba-diving...

What plants need

Like you, plants need air, food and water. Unlike you, they must also have sunlight. They will die without it. As soon as a young plant sprouts, it starts to open its leaves and take in the sunlight.

Reach for the sky

A tree will change its shape to catch as much sunlight as possible. Normally, leaves grow all around a tree. However, if a tree is surrounded by other trees, it cranes upwards to stop being shaded by its neighbours, so most of the leaves grow at the top. Trees standing together in a group tend to form a shape that looks almost like a single tree.

A copse (a small cluster of trees) can grow to look like a single tree, as each tree turns outwards to face the light.

Escape from the black box

Plant a raw runner bean in a pot of well-watered soil. Place it inside a box that has been painted black inside and fitted with cardboard barriers, as in the drawing. Leave the top flaps open a bit, to let in some light. The growing bean plant will twist and turn to find the light.

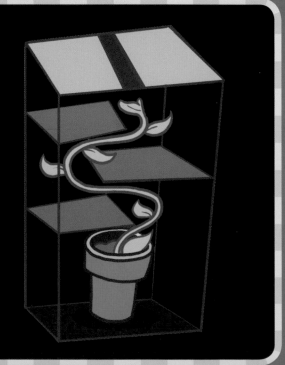

Roots

Down below the ground, a tree's roots search for water and **minerals**. There are plenty of roots down there, although you can't see most of them.

Tree roots are strong – they can push rocks apart, force their way into water pipes or push walls over. You often see bulges in pavements caused by their powerful growth.

Roots also anchor a plant in the ground, so that it can't be easily shifted by wind or floods.

Do you know of any impressive root growth near where you live? See page 30.

Tree root system

Many trees have root systems that are just as big and spread out as their branches are above ground.

Below: Roots don't move fast, but as they grow they push and heave at anything that's in their way.

Photosynthesis

Plants take in sunlight, air, water and minerals, and turn it into food so that they can live and grow. This process is called photosynthesis. It's what makes plants different from animals. While animals need to find food to eat, plants make their own food. It happens inside their leaves.

Leaf factories

The leaf is a very busy place. Air containing carbon dioxide is let in through tiny holes, called **stomata**, on the underside of the leaf. Water, along with some useful chemicals from the soil, is transported up from the ground along tubes inside the plant, called **xylem**.

Inside the plant's leaves are tiny factories called **chloroplasts**, which contain a chemical called chlorophyll. The choroplasts take in carbon dioxide from the air, and water and minerals from the soil, and use energy from the Sun to turn them into food. Waste oxygen gas comes out through the stomata. The food is carried to different parts of the plant along tubes called **phloem**.

Chlorophyll gives leaves their green colour. What gives you your colour? See page 30.

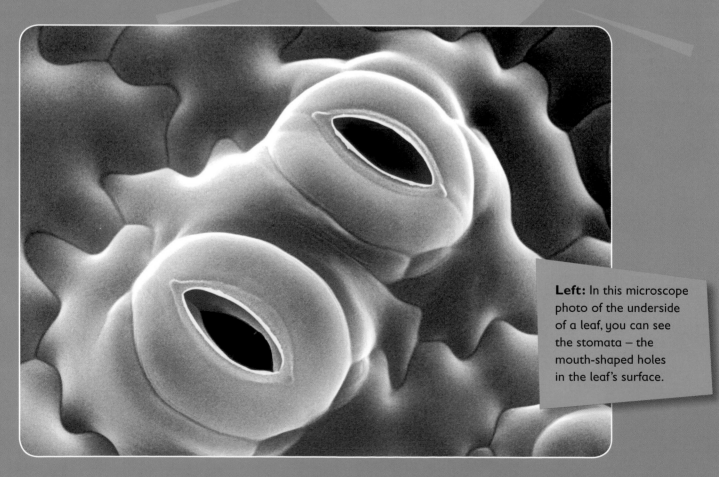

Left: In this microscope photo of the underside of a leaf, you can see the stomata — the mouth-shaped holes in the leaf's surface.

How photosynthesis works

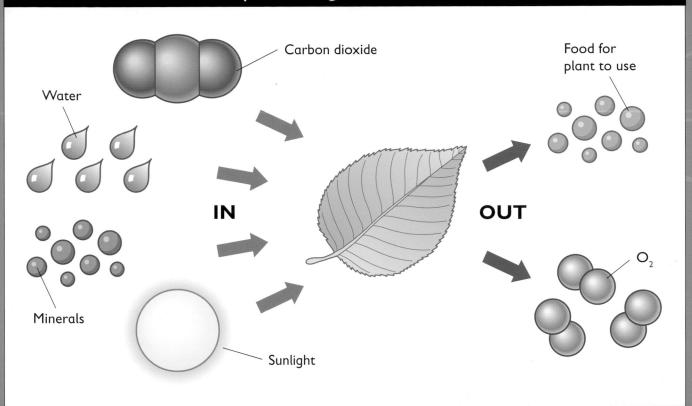

Carbon dioxide

Water

Minerals

Sunlight

IN

OUT

Food for plant to use

O_2

Gas swap

Carbon dioxide is a gas made from carbon and oxygen. We humans breathe out carbon dioxide as a waste gas. Plants like it, though, and if there is enough sunlight, they take in carbon dioxide and use it to make food. They give out oxygen as a waste product. This is handy for humans. Like all animals we need oxygen in the air we breathe.

20sq metres of garden

Above: An average-sized garden full of plants can provide all the oxygen that one human being needs. Luckily, even if you don't have a garden, there are millions of plants all over the world, in forests, fields and seas, providing enough oxygen for us all.

Water

A plant needs water. As well as being used in photosynthesis, water helps to keep plants upright. Without it, a plant will wilt and sag like an empty balloon.

Rooting for water

One of the main jobs for a plant's roots is to find and take in water. The roots are very serious about their task. A single ryegrass plant was found to have more than 14 billion root hairs! They had a surface area of more than 400 square metres. It seems incredible, but it's possible because the root hairs are microscopically small and cover the entire surface of the roots. This allows the roots to have as much contact with the damp soil as possible. Water seeps into the root hairs by a process called 'osmosis'.

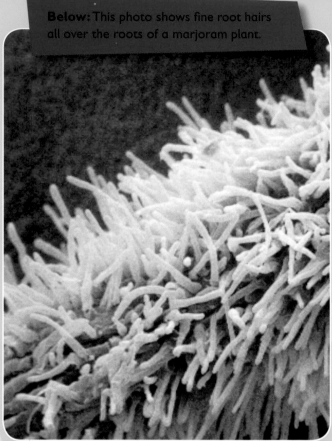

Below: This photo shows fine root hairs all over the roots of a marjoram plant.

Will future astronauts be able to grow plants where there is no gravity? What will happen to the plants? See page 30.

Water keeps a plant firm and upright, or 'turgid'. Without water, a plant becomes droopy.

Reaching down

One of the wonders of plants is that they know which way to grow. You can't grow a plant upside-down, because it can sense gravity. Even if you plant a seed upside-down, the root will turn down, and the stem will point up.

How does it work? Cells in the roots contain tiny, heavy grains, called **statoliths**. Pulled by gravity, the statoliths sink to the bottom of the cell, telling the root to grow in that direction.

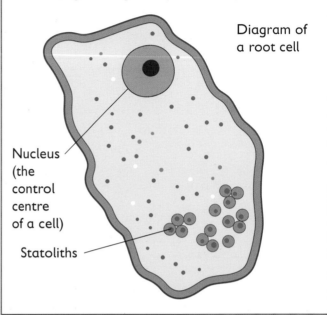

Statoliths

Statoliths tell a root cell which way is down, by sinking to the bottom of the cell.

Diagram of a root cell

Nucleus (the control centre of a cell)

Statoliths

Left: This never happens! Plants are designed to grow the right way up, so that their leaves can reach the light and their roots can reach water in the soil.

Drawing roots

As roots grow away from the base of a plant, they divide, then divide again, forming hundreds or even thousands of branches. This experiment lets you recreate this process.

First, take a piece of paper and fold it in half across its width, then again into thirds, as shown here. When you open it out, it will be divided into six bands. These represent the layers of soil beneath a plant.

Draw a single root in the top section. In the second section, divide it into two. In the third section, divide each of the new roots into two, and so on. How many roots do you have by the bottom of the page?

Minerals

When a plant's roots take in water, they also take in minerals from the soil, which they need to help them grow.

Soil bacteria

The minerals a plant needs are made by some very important friends of the plant which live close to its roots – soil bacteria. These are tiny living things, but what they lack in size they make up for in numbers. In one teaspoonful of soil there can be up to a billion bacteria. They feed on dead leaves and organic waste, turning it into minerals the plant can use.

Above: Soil bacteria turn kitchen waste into compost, which contains the essential minerals a plant needs to grow.

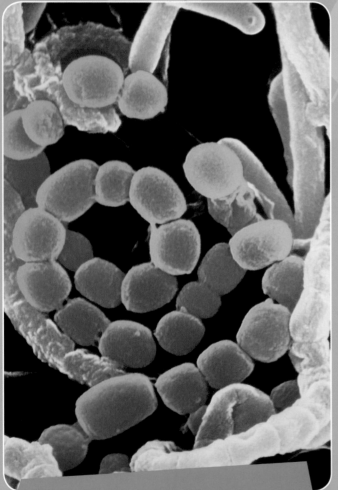

Above: The blob shapes in this picture are soil bacteria clustered around a plant root, magnified thousands of times.

How to make food disappear

Bury some fruit or vegetable waste in the garden and mark the spot.

Two weeks later, dig it up to see what remains. (Use gloves and a spade and wash your hands afterwards!) The food has decayed and partly disappeared because of the action of soil bacteria.

Sucking up

How do water and minerals travel around inside a plant? Plants contain tubes called 'xylem', which run from the roots to the leaves. In some plants, such as large trees, this can be a very long way. As the experiment to the right shows, it's difficult to suck water upwards over a long distance. But in a plant, the water is sucked up by a very clever system called 'transpiration'.

Water evaporates from the leaf, and as it does so it is replaced by water from the top end of the xylem tube. As this water moves upward, more water is drawn up from below. By this method, a plant is kept fed and watered from its roots.

Xylem tubes

Xylem tubes have to be strong, so that they don't collapse under the pressure of the sucking action from above. They are reinforced with a substance called lignin. Lignin is what makes wood hard and 'woody'.

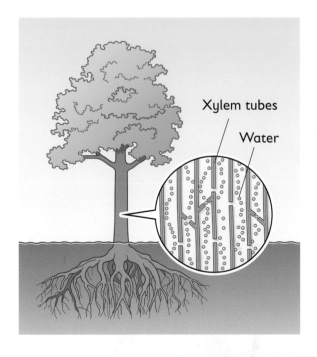

Xylem tubes

Water

Long straw

Fix several drinking straws together by inserting the end of one into the next, then sticking tape around the join. You may need to pinch the tip of each straw first. Keep going until you have a giant straw, as tall as you. Ask an adult to try sucking a drink through it. Now you know how hard it is to suck liquid up over a long distance, as a tree has to!

Plant parts

Like humans and animals, plants are made up of different parts, which all have different jobs to do to help the plant survive.

Cells

Like other living things, plants are made up of basic building blocks called cells. Different cells have different jobs. Leaf cells use their chloroplasts to make food, using sunlight. Phloem cells form phloem tubes that carry food all around the plant. Root cells build roots that grow downwards and take water into the plant. Xylem cells make xylem tubes that carry water up to the leaves. They also have thick, woody walls that help to keep the plant upright.

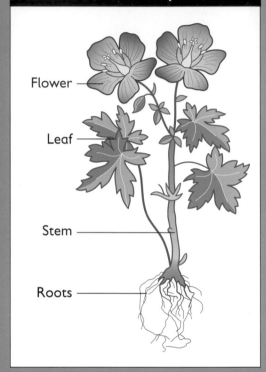

Parts of a plant

- Flower
- Leaf
- Stem
- Roots

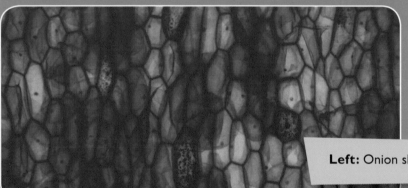

Left: Onion skin cells seen under a microscope.

How strong is a tree?

Roll a piece of paper into a tube. Stand it up to make a 'tree trunk'. Balance a book on it. Then another, and another. How many can you balance?

A tube is one of the strongest shapes for supporting weight. If you make any other shape from the paper, such as a tent or a cube, it will be much weaker. Plants form tube-shaped stems and trunks to give them as much strength as possible.

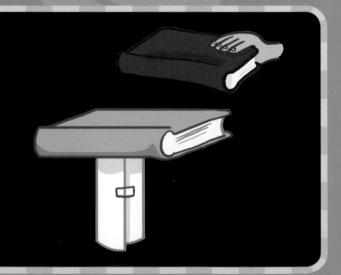

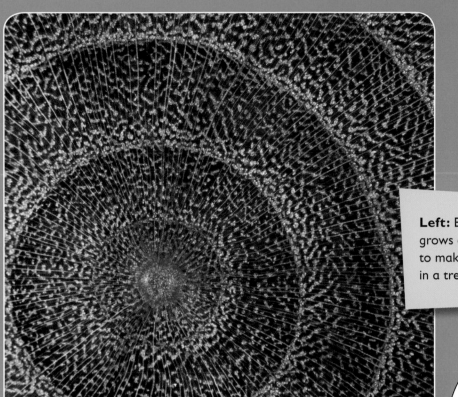

Can you see the cells in a real piece of onion skin? See page 30.

Left: Each year, as a tree grows taller, it grows a new ring of wood around its trunk to make itself stronger. The number of rings in a tree's trunk reveals its age.

Flowers

Flowers are often the most colourful and complicated parts of a plant, and they have an important job to do. Plants need to make seeds, which will grow into new plants. To do this, they must combine some of their cells with cells from other plants. But how can one plant reach another plant when they are stuck in the ground? The flower is their answer. Each flower contains a part called a **stamen**, which makes grains of **pollen**. It is when pollen grains from one flower join with another flower that seeds are made.

But how can one plant send its pollen to another? Some plants simply let their pollen float away on the wind. Others use insects to carry it. Turn the page to find out how.

Pollination

'Pollination' means spreading pollen grains from one flower to another, which helps plants to make seeds. Luckily for plants, pollination is something insects do very well.

Pollen post

Bees are great pollinators. They like to eat pollen, and also nectar, a sweet juice found inside flowers. While they are collecting their food, some of the pollen gets stuck to the their bodies. When they visit another flower of the same kind, the pollen rubs off onto the flower's **stigma**. The job is done!

When it lands on another flower's stigma, a pollen grain sends out a fine tube right down the stigma and **style** to the flower's **ovule**. The pollen's DNA (instructions for growing into a new plant) passes down the tube and joins with the flower's DNA in the ovule. It then starts to make a seed. Some flowers can make a million seeds in a single season.

Can you think of any other animals that might help to pollinate a flower? See page 30.

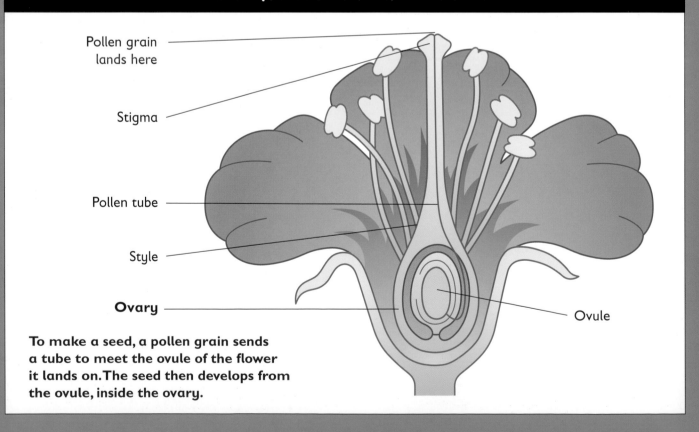

How flowers make seeds

Pollen grain lands here

Stigma

Pollen tube

Style

Ovary

Ovule

To make a seed, a pollen grain sends a tube to meet the ovule of the flower it lands on. The seed then develops from the ovule, inside the ovary.

Above: The hairs on this bee's body have picked up plenty of pollen, which it will carry to the next flower it visits.

Insect attractors

Using insects for pollination is so successful that flowers have developed many ways to attract bees, or other creatures that will help spread their pollen. They have brightly coloured petals so that insects can see them easily. They make sugary nectar to encourage insects to visit them for a meal, and they have strong scents to tempt insects to come and have a taste.

Some flowers, such as the corpse flower, smell of rotting meat. This is irresistible to flies. Other flowers disguise themselves as female bees to attract male bees, and all flowers have their stamens cleverly positioned, so that any visitors become well-covered with pollen.

Left: To humans, the rotting-flesh smell of the corpse flower is disgusting. However, it reminds flies of their favourite food, rotting meat, so they head towards it.

Seeds

Plants make seeds in order to reproduce (make new plants of the same type). One little seed, such as an acorn, contains all the information needed to grow a whole plant, such as an oak tree.

Ready to drop

Seeds are usually dry, to prevent them from rotting, and covered by a hard skin or shell, to try to prevent animals eating them (though many animals still do). Most plants release their seeds in autumn, ready to grow the following spring.

But just dropping the seeds straight down onto the ground is not much use. After all, there is already a plant growing there: the parent plant. It's much better for a plant to spread its family far and wide. To do this it must spread, or disperse, its seeds.

This looks like a nice place to put down roots!

Left: This burr contains seeds. Its tiny hooks hold onto animals' fur (or people's clothes) and the burr gets carried away from its parent plant to grow somewhere else.

Interesting seeds

Dandelion seeds have a fluffy 'parachute' that floats on winds and air currents.

Sycamore seeds have a wing that makes them spiral and fall slowly.

Cotton seeds have fluffy fibres to help the wind carry them.

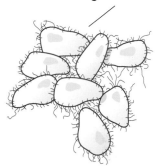

Balsam seeds come in pods that explode to throw their seeds out.

Seeds on the move

When an animal eats a fruit, such as an apple or a plum, it is doing exactly what the fruit tree wants. The fruit is tasty, but the pips (seeds) will go right through the creature and will be deposited somewhere far from the tree, where they may start to grow. Other seeds have tiny hooks all over them, which catch onto the fur of passing animals and hitch a lift far away.

Coconuts can float, so currents carry them across oceans to islands and faraway shores. Some seeds have fine hairs or wing-shaped parts, to help the wind to carry them away.

Humans can disperse, too! How many of your class or friends have family in other parts the world?

Designing seed dispersal systems

Use a paperclip as your 'seed'. Use a fan to make some 'wind' to disperse it. How can you help it travel a long way? You could attach a wing made of paper. What else might work?

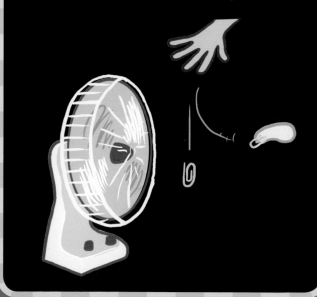

Growth

After being released from their plants, seeds are ready to start growing. But they can only grow if they have the right conditions – such as soil to grow in, and enough water and warmth. Many plants produce hundreds of seeds, to make sure that a few of them will find a good place to grow.

Germination

Once a seed is on a good patch of soil, it waits for the right season to **germinate**, or start growing. In the northern and southern hemispheres, this is usually spring, when the weather is warming up and the ground is damp. The seed sends down a fine root, which begins to take in water. There is a little bit of food in the seed, which the baby plant consumes as it swells with water. Soon it sends a shoot upwards, and the first tiny leaves begin to photosynthesize (see page 8). The new plant has begun to grow.

Some seeds can wait a very long time to find their 'spring'. Recently, seeds found tucked inside a 203-year-old book were planted. They sprouted nicely.

At the equator, there's no spring – just a rainy season and a dry season. What do you think seeds do there? See page 30.

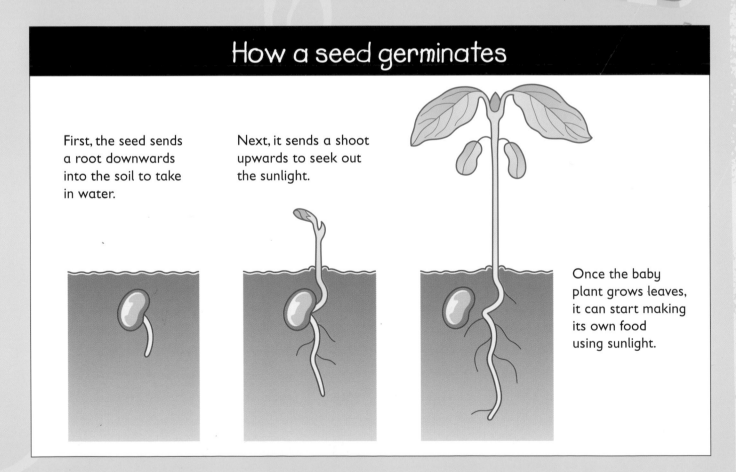

How a seed germinates

First, the seed sends a root downwards into the soil to take in water.

Next, it sends a shoot upwards to seek out the sunlight.

Once the baby plant grows leaves, it can start making its own food using sunlight.

Left: As winter approaches, the green chlorophyll in leaves is no longer needed. It breaks down, and the leaves turn red, yellow and brown, before falling off.

Plants in winter

In parts of the world that have four seasons, plant growth is strongest in spring and summer. As winter approaches, it's colder and there is less sunlight, so it's harder for plants to grow. The flowers and leaves have finished their work for the year, so lots of trees and plants shed their leaves in autumn.

Many plants stop growing over the winter. Some plants die, but they haven't stopped being useful. They join the leaves on the ground and rot away through the winter. The soil bacteria turn them back into minerals, which the next year's growing plants can use.

Where am I?

In 2005, botanists (plant scientists) planted an 2000-year-old date palm seed, dug up during excavations of King Herod's palace near the Dead Sea in Israel. The seed germinated and grew into a healthy plant! The plant was nicknamed Methuselah, after a very old character in the Bible.

How plants struggle

Plants can be found everywhere, from icy glaciers to the middle of the desert – places where humans find it very hard to live. But plants have lots of cunning tricks to help them survive.

Hot and cold

In very hot, dry places, such as deserts, there's not much water. To find the water they need, plants spread their roots very wide. When there is a rare shower of rain, the plant can quickly collect the water from a large area. Cacti in the desert store water in their thick stems. They have thick, waxy skin that prevents the water from escaping into the air.

Plants in extremely chilly places, such as the Arctic, have a similar thick skin to keep the cold at bay. Some pine trees can survive temperatures of -40°C, which would freeze your blood.

Can you think how you would solve the problems of living in very hot, cold or dry places? See page 31.

Above: A cactus has sharp spines (which are modified leaves) to stop thirsty animals from eating it. It also has thick stems because thin stems would allow too much water to escape.

Cactus roots

Under the ground, a saguaro cactus's roots spread out wider than the cactus is tall, to collect as much water as possible when it rains.

Staying safe

Plants also have to defend themselves against animals who want to eat them. Giraffes, elephants, goats and other plant-eaters have evolved necks, trunks and teeth specially to help them eat plants. Insects munch though plants' leaves, burrow into their flower buds or suck their sap.

Plants fight back with stings and thorns to keep the animals away, poisons that make them taste unpleasant, or even more dramatic defences. The rubber plant, for example, makes sticky latex (which we turn into useful rubber) in order to gum up the mouthparts of insects that try to feed on it. The bullhorn acacia goes one better. It lets fierce ants live inside its thorns and makes a special food for them on its leaves. In return, the ants fight off other insects and larger animals that try to eat the tree, by biting and stinging them.

Right: Giraffes evolved their long necks so that they could reach up to eat leaves from trees.

How plants compete

As if it isn't enough to be frozen or fried by the weather, or eaten alive by animals, plants also do battle with each other. All of them are trying to get as much light, water and minerals as they can – and they don't like other plants being in their way.

Fighting for space

Plants try to avoid each other's shadow by growing upwards. The tallest trees, giant redwoods, can reach over 100m tall. Some sneaky plants, such as ivy, use tall trees to climb up so that they can reach the sunlight themselves.

Some plants grow huge leaves to put the plants beneath them in the shade. Others grow long thin stalks to reach through to the light.

Plants also battle for space underground. The ground elder has underground stems that stifle the roots of other plants. Some plants, such as the rhododendron, make the soil poisonous to other types of plants.

And all plants send their seeds as far away as possible, to take over new territory. To make sure they produce enough seeds, they make as many flowers as possible, and compete to make the most attractive flowers for bees to visit.

Above: Rainforests are thick forests found in warm, wet, tropical parts of the world. They contain a huge variety of plants, all struggling to find the light, food and water they need.

Watch plants compete

Fill a small plant pot with compost, and plant six seeds close together (you can get seeds such as beetroot or carrot seeds from a gardening shop). Water the pot regularly and keep it in a sunny place.

As the seeds start to germinate and grow, watch what happens. Do all six grow? Of the plants that appear, do they look different from each other? In any batch of seeds, some will be stronger and healthier than others, and will win the struggle to survive.

Below: Gardeners try to encourage and help the plants they want — such as vegetables, fruit trees and flowers — while killing and removing plants they don't want — 'weeds'.

Many weeds are actually very pretty. Can you think of any? See page 31.

What is a weed?

As any gardener knows, weeds will grab any chance they can to grow, choking other plants and stealing their space. But weeds aren't a different or special kind of plant. They're just normal plants that gardeners and farmers don't want around. Like any other plant, they struggle to survive and compete with other plants to get what they need.

Right: The strangler fig survives by wrapping itself around the trunk of another tree and stealing its water, while smothering the branches with its leaves. Eventually the host tree dies, leaving the hollow strangler fig standing alone.

How we use plants

Plants are incredibly important to humans. As well as adding oxygen to the air we breathe (see page 5), they provide us with food, fabrics, medicines and many other things.

Plant products

Plants are central to our diet. If we are vegetarian, we eat mainly plants. If we are meat-eaters, we eat animals, too, but those animals eat plants. We burn plants for heat and energy, either as wood, or as coal and oil, which are made of ancient, decomposed plants. We wear plants – flax plants can be turned into linen, and cotton plants into cotton thread. The paper used to make this book came from trees. We have used plants for medicines for thousands of years. Palm leaves and bamboo can be used to make hats, baskets, mats and roofs. Bamboo is so strong it is even used to make houses and scaffolding.

How many plant-based objects can you find around you? See page 31.

Below: Large, sturdy plants such as trees and bamboo have been used for thousands of years to make human homes.

Breeding useful plants

Modern crops, such as wheat and apples, have been developed and bred from wild versions that provide much less food.

Wild grass

Modern wheat

Wild crabapples

Modern apple

Plant control

Over time, humans have changed plants to suit our needs. The seed heads of some types of grass might remind you of an ear of wheat. The two are indeed related. Thousands of years ago, people learned how to select the most useful kinds of grass, and breed them together to create crop grasses which we now call wheat, rice, barley or rye. Nearly all modern fruits and vegetables began as rather small and bitter-tasting fruits, and were made tasty over centuries by carefully selecting and breeding the best plants.

Today, scientists can also modify plants by changing their DNA (the instructions inside their cells that tell them how to live and grow). This can create completely new, genetically modified or 'GM' plants. For example, scientists have created a type of GM cotton plant that poisons a cotton pest called the bollworm.

Below: Scientists have made GM strawberry plants that can resist frost. They combined strawberry plant DNA with DNA from a cold-water fish that helps it to survive in freezing cold water.

keeping it green

We depend on plants for our food. Because the world's population is growing, there are more and more mouths to feed. So we are always looking for ways to get more crops from the ground.

Chemical crops

We plant more and more crops wherever we can find space. To keep the ground full of minerals, we can no longer just wait for bacteria to decompose vegetation to make compost, so we add man-made fertilizers to the ground. We also use weedkillers to kill rival plants, and pesticides to deal with insects and animals that might eat our crops. Modern fields therefore have many strange chemicals in them. Today, many farmers have to be good chemists as well.

Right: You should wash fruit and vegetables before eating them, as they may have chemicals such as pesticides on them, or bacteria from the soil.

Left: Some farmers have fields so large that the easiest way to spray them with chemicals is from a plane.

Above: Tree roots hold the soil in place, especially on hillsides. Many landslides have happened after trees were cut down to make space for crops.

Saving the forests

To make space for more fields of crops, we burn or cut down forests and jungles. But we must be careful. We need trees to provide wood, to hold the soil together with their roots, and to add oxygen to the air we breathe in. So governments everywhere are encouraging the planting of new forests, in an effort to keep the planet healthy.

There is also a movement to grow crops without artificial fertilizers, pesticides and weedkillers, in order to protect the Earth's soil and wildlife, and keep dangerous chemicals out of our food. This is known as organic farming. Organic food is becoming increasingly popular.

Ask an adult about what chemicals they put on their garden. See page 31.

Questions and answers

Have you noticed any plants in unusual places? (page 5)

Look for them growing on the roofs of buildings, between bricks in walls, or in roadside gutters. Look for green algae or moss on rocks. Plants grow in the strangest places!

Do you know of any impressive root growth near where you live? (page 7)

Think of the walk to school, or to the park. Many tree roots affect the man-made structures around them, such as walls, roads or pavements.

Chlorophyll gives leaves their green colour. What gives you your colour? (page 8)

Human skin colour comes from a combination of melanin, a brown pigment in the skin, and the red blood beneath the skin.

Will future astronauts be able to grow plants where there is no gravity? What will happen to the plants? (page 10)

Astronauts have taken seeds into space to find out how well plants can grow there. They have found that the lack of gravity and the shortage of sunlight can make plants confused and affects how well they grow.

Can you see the cells in a piece of onion skin? (page 15)

The cells of a single onion layer can be seen with the naked eye, but a magnifying glass will help.

Can you think of any other animals that might help to pollinate a flower? (page 16)

Any animals that feed from inside flowers, such as hummingbirds, butterflies, moths and even small lizards, can be pollinators. Larger animals, such as cows, tend not to be because they eat the whole plant.

At the equator, there's no spring – just a rainy season and a dry season. What do you think seeds do there? (page 20)

At the equator, seeds usually germinate right at the start of the rainy season so they get lots of water.

Can you think how you would solve the problems of living in very hot, cold or dry places? (page 22)

People do live in extreme conditions. They learn how to find water in the desert by digging underground or extracting water from plants. In cold regions, people use animal furs or modern fabrics to keep warm. Instead of wheeled vehicles, they use snowmobiles.

Many weeds are actually very pretty. Can you think of any? (page 25)

Buttercups, daisies and dandelions are good examples.

How many plant-based objects can you find around you? (page 26)

Try looking at your clothes, books, baskets, rugs, chairs, buildings, stairs, cushions, string, toys and pencils.

Ask an adult about the chemicals they put on their garden. (page 29)

Another way to find out about the chemicals we use on our gardens is to look around a gardening shop.

Glossary

Atmosphere – The layer of gases surrounding the Earth.

Bacteria – Tiny, single-celled living things which live all around us.

Carbon dioxide – A gas found in the air. Plants take it in during photosynthesis.

Chloroplasts – Tiny green capsules in leaf cells which use sunlight to turn carbon dioxide and water into molecules for building and feeding the plant.

Cyanobacteria – The very earliest form of life on Earth, from which all plants evolved.

Germination – When a seed starts to grow into a plant.

Minerals – Chemicals in the ground. Plants use various minerals, or mineral salts (chemicals containing minerals) to help them grow.

Ovary – The part of a flower where seeds are created from an ovule and pollen.

Ovule – The part of a flower which will develop into a seed when fertilized by pollen.

Oxygen – Gas that plants give out as a waste product, and which is breathed in by animals.

Phloem – Tubes that transport food in a plant.

Photosynthesis – The process by which a plant uses water, carbon dioxide and sunlight to make its 'food' – all the energy and building materials it needs.

Pollen – Tiny powdery grains which contain a plant's DNA. Pollen combines with ovules to make seeds.

Stamen – The part of a flower which makes pollen.

Statoliths – Tiny grains found in plant roots that are pulled downwards by gravity and therefore tell a root which way to grow.

Stigma – The part of a flower which receives pollen from other flowers.

Stomata – Tiny pores, or holes, that allow carbon dioxide into a leaf, where it is used to make food during photosynthesis.

Style – The stalk connecting the stigma to the ovary.

Xylem – Woody tubes which carry water up a plant from the ground to the leaves.

Index